HEALTHY HABITS

EXERCISING

by Emma Carlson Berne

Consultant: Beth Gambro
Reading Specialist, Yorkville, Illinois

Minneapolis, Minnesota

Teaching Tips

Before Reading

- Look at the cover of the book. Discuss the picture and the title.
- Ask readers to brainstorm a list of what they already know about exercising. What can they expect to see in the book?
- Go on a picture walk, looking through the pictures to discuss vocabulary and make predictions about the text.

During Reading

- Read for purpose. Encourage readers to think about exercising habits as they are reading.
- Ask readers to look for the details of the book. What are they learning about how to exercise in a way that is healthy?
- If readers encounter an unknown word, ask them to look at the sounds in the word. Then, ask them to look at the rest of the page. Are there any clues to help them understand?

After Reading

- Encourage readers to pick a buddy and reread the book together.
- Ask readers to name two reasons to make exercising a habit. Find the pages that tell about these things.
- Ask readers to write or draw something they learned about exercising.

Credits:
Cover and title page, © truenos86/Shutterstock; 3, © Kenishirotie/Shutterstock; 5, © imtmphoto/Shutterstock; 7, © JackF/Adobe Stock; 8-9, © Pixel-Shot/Adobe Stock; 11, © FatCamera/iStock; 12-13, © Imgorthand/iStock; 14-15, © CandyRetriever/iStock; 16-17, © BraunS/iStock; 18-19, © famveldman/Adobe Stock; 21, © Robert Kneschke/Adobe Stock; 22T, © andresr/iStock; 22M, © Amorn Suriyan/Shutterstock; 22B, © staticnak1983/iStock; 23TL, © monkeybusinessimages/iStock; 23TM, © pick-uppath/iStock; 23TR, © PeopleImages/iStock, © Shanvood/Shutterstock; 23BL, © Deepak Sethi/iStock, © Lucia Fox/Shutterstock; 23BM, © SDI Productions/iStock; 23BR, © FatCamera/iStock.

STATEMENT ON USAGE OF GENERATIVE ARTIFICIAL INTELLIGENCE
Bearport Publishing remains committed to publishing high-quality nonfiction books. Therefore, we restrict the use of generative AI to ensure accuracy of all text and visual components pertaining to a book's subject. See BearportPublishing.com for details.

Library of Congress Cataloging-in-Publication Data

Names: Berne, Emma Carlson, 1979- author.
Title: Exercising / by Emma Carlson Berne.
Description: Bearcub books. | Minneapolis, Minnesota : Bearport Publishing
   Company, [2024] | Series: Healthy habits | "Consultant: Beth Gambro,
   Reading Specialist, Yorkville, Illinois." | Includes bibliographical references and index.
Identifiers: LCCN 2023028244 (print) | LCCN 2023028245 (ebook) | ISBN
   9798889162452 (library binding) | ISBN 9798889162520 (paperback) | ISBN
   9798889162582 (ebook)
Subjects: LCSH: Exercise for children--Juvenile literature. | Outdoor
   recreation for children--Juvenile literature.
Classification: LCC GV443 .B397 2024 (print) | LCC GV443 (ebook) | DDC
   613.7/1083--dc23/eng/20230726
LC record available at https://lccn.loc.gov/2023028244
LC ebook record available at https://lccn.loc.gov/2023028245

Copyright © 2024 Bearport Publishing Company. All rights reserved. No part of this publication may be reproduced in whole or in part, stored in any retrieval system, or transmitted in any form or by any means, electronic, mechanical, photocopying, recording, or otherwise, without written permission from the publisher.
For more information, write to Bearport Publishing, 5357 Penn Avenue South, Minneapolis, MN 55419.

Contents

Zoom! 4

Make It a Habit 22

Glossary 23

Index 24

Read More 24

Learn More Online 24

About the Author 24

Zoom!

I go fast on my bike.

Whee!

Riding my bike is good exercise.

It helps me stay healthy.

Say exercise like EK-sur-*size*

I exercise to keep my body strong.

It is something I do every day.

That makes it a **habit**!

There are many ways to exercise.

I can go on walks with my family.

Playing sports is fun, too.

Exercising gives me strong **muscles**.

It makes my bones strong, too.

Together, muscles and bones help me grow big.

When I exercise, my **heart** goes fast.

Thump-thump, thump-thump!

It gets stronger.

My **lungs** do, too.

They help me breathe.

Exercising gives me **energy**.

It keeps me going all day.

Moving can also make me feel better.

It helps me relax.

I make sure to stay safe when I exercise.

Stretching helps my body get ready to move.

I drink water as I go.

It is easy to add exercise to my day.

I stretch first thing when I wake up.

Sometimes, I bike to school.

Exercising makes me feel good.

It is great to move every day.

Let's make exercising a habit!

Make It a Habit

A habit is something you do every day. What are ways we can make exercising a habit?

Make it fun! Try a new sport.

You can exercise anywhere! Try jumping rope in your yard.

Find a buddy to exercise with. Then, get moving together!

Glossary

energy the power to do things, such as work or run

habit something done regularly

heart the part of the body that pumps blood

lungs the parts of the body that are used for breathing

muscles the parts of the body that help you move

stretching pulling a muscle to make it longer

Index

bones 10
habit 6, 20, 22
heart 12
lungs 12
muscles 10
sports 8, 22
stretch 17, 19
water 17

Read More

Gaertner, Meg. *Getting Exercise (Taking Care of Myself)*. Mendota Heights, MN: Little Blue Readers, 2022.

Gleisner, Jenna Lee. *Exercising (First Routines)*. Minneapolis: Jump!, 2023.

Learn More Online

1. Go to **www.factsurfer.com** or scan the QR code below.
2. Enter **"Healthy Habits Exercising"** into the search box.
3. Click on the cover of this book to see a list of websites.

About the Author

Emma Carlson Berne lives with her family in Cincinnati, Ohio. Horseback riding is her favorite way to exercise.